I0397028

A Moment for Success

power-ups for busy people

101 free ways to reduce
stress, increase creativity,
enhance productivity,
improve health, and
achieve success
in 30 seconds.

Alice Langholt, MJS

ISBN-13: 978-1545549612
ISBN-10: 1545549613

DEDICATION

I dedicate this book to the person who supports my work, no matter where my creativity takes me, every day – my husband, Evan. Thank you for loving me, and for being my partner on this incredible journey.

HOW TO USE THIS BOOK

The key to success is in 30 second moments...

The mind, emotions, and body are all linked. And, the way to balance all of them begins with the mind.

Choose any page. Read and do the 30 second task on that page. You will find your stress levels decrease, and your confidence, creativity, and optimism elevate, as you become empowered to greater levels of personal achievement and better health.

In these pages, you'll find:
Inspiring affirmations, vivid visualizations, 30-second brainstorming sessions, mindfulness practices, physical stretches designed to release block-causing mental stress, and more.

Everything can be completed in 30 seconds with lasting benefits.

Greater success is just 30 seconds away.

The Model You

In these 30 seconds, imagine the best, most self-assured, successful version of yourself sitting in a chair across from you. Use as much detail as you can, from dress to posture, appearance, demeanor, etc.

Then, move into that chair. Imagine absorbing the energy of that Model You.

Take on that persona as yours, **because it is.**

Find the Meaning

A Harvard study showed that employees who feel that the work they do is meaningful are happier at work. Use these 30 seconds to list as many ways as you can that your work has a meaningful and positive impact.

After this exercise, notice the difference in how you feel.

Strike a Pose

Research shows that your posture affects your confidence and how you are perceived. Striking a confident pose reduces stress and increases testosterone, a confidence-boosting hormone in the male and female bodies.

For 30 seconds, stand like a super hero - chest out, hands on your hips!

Bring that super hero feeling into the rest of your day.

Say Affirmations

To realign yourself with positive energy which attracts more goodness into your life, and helps increase optimism, say each of these aloud and with feeling:

I learn from every experience.

Every outcome reveals new opportunities.

I am capable of greatness.

Wisdom Break

Access and express some of your accumulated wisdom. Surprise! You're wise!

Write your answers to:

3 things I've learned about having a positive outlook.

ALICE LANGHOLT

Ask Yourself

Breathe for 10 seconds, and ask yourself:

What would I need to change to become more of who I aspire to be?

Write your answer below.

Just for Today

Thank someone who has helped you. Be specific about what that person did and how it made your life or job easier that time.

Expressing appreciation is a trait of successful people.

Declutter

An organized work space helps the mind think more clearly. In these 30 seconds, clear a space or reorganize something around you.

Notice the clarity of thought that follows.

Embody Your Best

Our self-image comes from how we define ourselves. Take 3 sticky notes. On the BOTTOM of each, write an adjective that, if you could say, "I want to be more _____" would fit. For example, "Ambitious," "Successful," or "Happy." Note: Only write the adjective (do not write, "I want…"). Write a different word on each piece of paper.

Then, above each of the words you wrote, write, "I am."

Post these notes around your workspace where you can easily see them.

Say Affirmations

To realign yourself with positive energy which attracts more goodness into your life, and helps increase optimism, say each of these aloud and with feeling:

I attract successful people.

I am deserving of abundance.

As I focus on success, more comes into my life.

Start at the End

Think of a goal you have, and picture yourself already having reached it. This has been proven to be more effective than constantly striving.

Start with the end goal, and then map out the steps to getting there.

Having a plan relieves stress and increases productivity.

If You Could

Imagine that you could have your boss' job for one day. Visualize what you would change about the way the company operates, how you would speak to people who work for you, what your office would look like, and what leadership qualities you have that you would bring to the position.

Afterward, ask yourself how you can nurture those leadership qualities in yourself now, and how you can apply these qualities to realize your goals.

Write Your Elevator Speech

The most successful people can clearly describe their work in 30 seconds. Write and memorize your 30 second job description and you'll be ready to network.

Networking is a key bridge to more success.

Say Affirmations

To realign yourself with positive energy which attracts more goodness into your life, and helps increase optimism, say each of these aloud and with feeling:

I am true to my values.

I set an example of excellence.

I attract the best into my life.

Take a Brain Break

The mind can only function well on complex tasks for a limited time. Breaks are important to restore mental clarity.

For these 30 seconds, get up and walk. Practice deep, conscious breathing.

Then come back and start fresh.

Be a Mentor

When we teach others, we express our wisdom in a way that makes someone's day better. It's a win-win.

How can you be a role model today?

Choose an action and do it!

If You Could

Imagine that you were a customer coming into your place of work. See the experience through the customer's eyes. Who would help this person? What would this person see and do? How would this person be treated, and his or her needs met? What would your role be in helping this person?

Afterward, reflect on how this experience helped you understand your company.

Is there anything you would change to better serve your customer base?

Say Affirmations

To realign yourself with positive energy which attracts more goodness into your life, and helps increase optimism, say each of these aloud and with feeling:

Every day, I grow more into the person I aspire to be.

My skills and knowledge make success a certainty.

I am productive and focused.

Toot Your Horn

Think of a moment in which you excelled. Share it now, either on social media, or with your colleagues.

Being proud of your work shows you as confident and successful. (It's good for your self-esteem too!)

Ask Yourself

Breathe for 10 seconds, and ask yourself:

How would I improve my business if given a chance?

Write your answer below.

Just for Today

Studies show that the physical act of smiling releases neuropeptides that increase confidence and positivity.

Smile right now for at least five seconds, and make it a point to smile at three people today.

Wisdom Break

Access and express some of your accumulated wisdom. Surprise! You're wise!

Write your answers to:

3 things I've learned about feeling confident.

Go for the Long Shot

So many times we think that big dreams are out of our reach. That self-limiting belief stops us from taking a chance.

Today, decide to reach outside your comfort zone and send an email, do an application, or make an inquiry call that will scare and excite you with the possibility of "What if?"

Just for Today

Freshen your workspace by changing or adding an inspiring or decorative item.

Change is good for sparking creativity, which affects your work for the better.

If You Could

Imagine that you work for your biggest competitor's company. What is different about the work environment, the products, the customer's experience?

See yourself there. What are you doing? What's your work like?

Afterward, reflect on what you might learn from your competition that you can take to improve anything about where you are now.

Wisdom Break

Access and express some of your accumulated wisdom. Surprise! You're wise!

Write your answers to:

3 things I've learned about being organized.

Support Success

Far beyond the scratching each other's back idea is the mentality that when those on your team, and those who you supervise, succeed, you succeed.

Today, do something that ensures the success of the team.

Wisdom Break

Access and express some of your accumulated wisdom. Surprise! You're wise!

Write your answers to:

3 things I've learned about ethical business practices.

Say Affirmations

To realign yourself with positive energy which attracts more goodness into your life, and helps increase optimism, say each of these aloud and with feeling:

I am confident in my abilities and intelligence.

I focus on solutions.

I am capable of handling all of my responsibilities.

Invite Noise In

A study published in the 2012 *Journal of Consumer Research* found that moderate ambient noise enhanced performance on creative tasks.

So, choose some background music, adjust the volume, and notice how it helps your flow of ideas.

Unwind Yourself

Stress from the day can keep a hold on you, even when you are home with your partner.

Take 30 seconds and **make a conscious choice to release the stress before you come into the house, allowing yourself to fully enjoy the experience of being together.**

Suggestion: imagine the stressors of your day as ropes around you. Untie yourself and drop them around your feet. Step out of the ropes and in the door.

Get a Mentor

No one succeeds alone. If you don't have a mentor, find one.

If you have a mentor, do something today that your mentor inspired you to try.

Make a Stop List

Removing bad habits from your life helps you achieve more, and become more positive.

On a piece of paper, write, "I will stop …." and write five things you will stop doing. Examples: procrastinating, worrying, eating junk food.

Post the list where you can see it.

When you've stopped doing the things on the list, cross them off and add something else.

The Top Three

Prioritizing helps you bring the most value to your productivity.

Use these 30 seconds to list your top three priorities for today, and then get to work with renewed motivation.

Ask Yourself

Breathe for 10 seconds, and ask yourself:

Who is my role model, and why?

What admirable qualities of this person can I adapt to increase my success?

Write your answer below.

Wisdom Break

Access and express some of your accumulated wisdom. Surprise! You're wise!

Write your answers to:

3 things I've learned about making a good impression.

Say Affirmations

To realign yourself with positive energy which attracts more goodness into your life, and helps increase optimism, say each of these aloud and with feeling:

I communicate with honesty and kindness.

I expect the best and it comes to me easily.

I am capable of achieving my highest aspirations.

Spinal Release

Improve your posture, and release stress and muscle tension in 30 seconds:

Sitting or standing, turn your torso around, and try to look over the opposite shoulder. Hold that position for three breaths.

Change sides and repeat.

Take a five second break and do each turn once more, as described.

Notice how you feel afterward.

Ask Yourself

Breathe for 10 seconds, and ask yourself:

What inspires me?

Write your answer below.

What We Focus on Grows Stronger

You have the power to change your day by changing your focus.

Look at your hand. Focus on it for five seconds.

Notice how your focused attention moved every other thought or concern to the background.

Now, think of your latest accomplishment. Focus entirely on this thought for 30 seconds.

Notice the confident and successful feelings that result.

If You Could

Imagine the perfect day at your job. Get into as much detail as you can, from walking in, through the whole day. What would make the day be "perfect" for you? What elements would need to happen for you to feel this way?

Afterward, consider the perfect moments you imagined.

What can you do to bring more of them into your day at work?

What would you need to change to have more "perfect" days at work?

Just for Today

No negative self-talk. Don't insult yourself in any way.

If you catch yourself saying something negative, immediately say something positive about yourself.

Breathe

Breathing deeply reduces stress, increases circulation, and increases clarity of thought.

Put your hand just beneath your navel. Breathe in slowly and fully, so that your hand rises as your lower abdomen expands.

Release the breath and feel your lower abdomen move back in towards your body.

Continue with full, mindful breaths at your own pace for 30 seconds and note how relaxed and stress-free you feel.

Know Yourself

Use this 30 seconds to ask yourself:

> When is my best time of day to work?

> What do I like to have around me to feel comfortable, positive, and productive?

> What are my favorite tools for getting work done?

> What time of day is it typically hardest to focus?

> Who do I like to turn to for support?

Once you've answered these questions, structure your day's tasks accordingly, and create the environment to support your best work.

Just for Today

Be aware of your posture. Hold your shoulders straight and your spine upright.

Confident posture creates and reinforces a confident attitude.

As your body, so your mind.

Invigorate Your Body and Mind

Here's a quick exercise break can get your blood flowing, release muscle tension, and generate mental clarity.

Do 10 of each of these:

> 1) Jumping jacks or marches in place with swinging arms.
>
> 2) Full arm circles forward and backward.
>
> 3) Reach high over your head with alternating arms.

Breathe and notice how good you feel afterward.

Become a Rock Star

Think of the person you admire most, whether you are personally acquainted or not.

List the three qualities you admire most about this person.

Now, choose one of these qualities.

What do you need to do or learn to adopt this quality into your life or develop it more? Answer this question, and take one step to put it into action. Choose a class, a book, or a means to develop this quality in yourself.

Do it in 10 Minutes

Set the timer for 10 minutes, and choose a task on your to-do list.

When we give ourselves a challenge to race the clock, we tend to work in spurts of motivated, productive, focused flow.

Get your timer ready, choose your task, and GO!

Wisdom Break

Access and express some of your accumulated wisdom. Surprise! You're wise!

Write your answers to:

3 things I've learned about success.

Thank You

Studies show that saying, "Thank you" is not only rewarding for the person who hears it, it gives a boost to the self-esteem of the person expressing it. Also, the workplace dynamics improve when people feel appreciated.

Start with YOU. Use these 30 seconds to list three things you did well so far today. Then thank yourself for them.

For the rest of today, sprinkle "Thank you" liberally into your conversations.

If You Could

Imagine that you are writing an anonymous letter to a newly hired coworker at your place of business. What frank advice would you give to help the person be successful and acclimate quickly to the new position?

Write this letter in your mind now.

Afterward, consider:

- What advice did you give that you couldn't tell someone straight out?
- What advice would have helped you most when you were new?
- How can you communicate the best of this advice in a positive and productive way?
- What pieces of advice would help YOU now?

Be Positive

The work is the same, whether you are dragged down by it, or take it as a challenge and are ready to do your best.

Having a positive attitude inspires others, and also makes tasks feel easier to accomplish, (so they will be).

You'll find yourself more productive, less stressed, and less tired out afterward if you can focus on being positive. For these 30 seconds, give yourself a pep talk. Then tackle that project. You can do it!

Boost Your Energy

These three weird techniques can give you a quick burst of mental energy. Try them now.

For 10 seconds each:

> 1. Pull your earlobes down three times.

> 2. Rub your tongue against the roof of your mouth for five seconds.

> 3. Stand on tiptoe and back down three times.

How different do you feel?

Wisdom Break

Access and express some of your
accumulated wisdom. Surprise! You're wise!

Write your answers to:

3 things I've learned about leadership.

Read for Pleasure

Reading for fun is entertaining and enriching. It also makes you a more interesting and well-rounded person.

What do you like to read?

For this 30 seconds, go online to Amazon.com, GoodReads.com, or the library, search for something that interests you - and get it.

Let it Go

We tend to be our harshest critics, beating ourselves up for each mistake - long after it's been made. Forgiveness helps us improve confidence and move forward.

1. Put your hands on your heart. Take a deep breath. Release.
2. Think of someone who wronged you. Say or think, "I forgive you, I can let this go now." Take a deep breath and release.
3. Think of something you are mad at yourself over. Say, "I forgive myself, I can let this go now."
4. With another deep breath, release it all.

Note how much lighter you feel.

Say Affirmations

To realign yourself with positive energy which attracts more goodness into your life, and helps increase optimism, say each of these aloud and with feeling:

I radiate enthusiasm.

I have the power to accomplish everything I need to do today.

I am energized.

Just for Today

Do something helpful for another person. Don't wait for a reason. Think of something that will make someone's day easier, and do it without being asked.

You'll both feel good, and that goodness creates ripples far into the future.

Refresh Your Eyes

Reduce eye strain from computers and reading small type. This exercise has also been known to improve vision.

Sit with your head straight, facing forward. Put your hands into fists resting on your knees, with thumbs pointing upward.

Do each exercise first on the right, then the left, closing your eyes for 5 seconds between them. Do not move your head for these exercises.

1. Look down at your thumb. Slowly rotate your thumb in a circle clockwise five times, then counter-clockwise five times.
2. (5 second break with eyes closed).
3. Slowly raise your arm, bringing your thumb upward above your head and then back down three times. Watch your thumb.

Blink and notice the difference.

List Your Accomplishments

Make a list of the tasks you've accomplished in the past year. Let it be a running list.

Include figures that illustrate your work, dedication, and achievements.

Not only is this exercise good for your self-esteem, but it can be material to support your candidacy for a promotion, pay increase, or for your resume.

Start that list now.

30 Second Meditation

Meditation has benefits to the body, mind, and emotions. Here's a simple and powerful one:

Quiet your breathing and sit still for 30 seconds. Try to hear, feel and experience your heart beating. Your heartbeat is part of your everyday life.

Bringing your awareness to the subtlety of its beating helps you appreciate the miracle of your life. It also calms the mind, enabling a higher level of focus afterward.

Grow Yourself

The Internet is a vast resource of information to help you develop skills that move you ahead in your career.

Think of one skill you'd like to develop further.

Use this 30 seconds to find an article, video, online course, book, or TED Talk that will help you get ahead.

Save it, and mark off time to give it your attention.

Ask, "What's Next?"

When issues arise, we can lament and assign blame, or we can get right to solution mode.

Using the two word phrase, "What's next?" can help you immediately begin the process of objective problem solving, to make the most positive and productive use of your time.

Successful people are problem solvers.

Be Here Now

Being present improves our communication, amplifies mental clarity, and helps increase productivity.

Today, focus on being mentally involved in this moment only.

Check yourself when your mind wanders and bring your awareness back to only what is happening now.

Repeat as often as needed to make it a habit.

Put Yourself on Your Calendar

Take out your calendar.

Block out an hour within the next three days. Schedule "Me Time" in that space.

This is now your sacred time, uninterrupted, to use as you please.

When that time comes, do whatever you feel like doing at that moment! Ideas: nap, watch a show you like, take a walk, exercise, take yourself to lunch, read for pleasure.

Now, and until that time, know it's just for you, and allow yourself to enjoy anticipating that gift you just gave yourself - Me Time - because you deserve it.

You're an Influence

Think for a moment of five people who've influenced your life for the better.

Next, choose one of them who may not know how much of an impact he or she has made. The person might be a famous writer or poet, or someone you know or knew personally.

Now, think of yourself. Realize that to some people YOU are this influential person. You're the one who makes a difference because of something you said, did or wrote that changed their lives for the better.

Soak it in. It's true. You matter, and you keep on making a difference every day.

Wisdom Break

Access and express some of your accumulated wisdom. Surprise! You're wise!

Write your answers to:

3 things I've learned about working with others.

Mind Dump

Ideas often pop up when we are actively engaged in something else.

Bring your idea flow front and center by using these 30 seconds to write down as many ideas and reminders as you can.

Don't worry if they're not related or disconnected. Just get them down. This process will keep you on top of things, and renew your mental focus afterward.

Get Outside

Fresh air and a change of scenery clears your mind, wakes you up and refreshes your perspective.

Use this 30 seconds (longer if you can) to get outside. Walk around, breathe deeply, and become reacquainted with the beautiful world.

Just for Today

Make a connection. Reach out via phone, text, or social media to someone you admire and make an appointment to meet or speak with each other.

Get it Done

Complaining and stressing often takes more time than the job itself.

Use these 30 seconds to decide on an action plan for your biggest, most unpleasant task, then buckle down and get to work.

You'll be surprised how much easier it goes than you anticipated.

Stress Begone

Stress can't coexist with confidence.

Think of your biggest challenge right now for 10 seconds.

Then say three times "**I got this.**"

- The 1st time, put your hand on your solar plexus.

- 2nd time, put your hand on your heart.

- 3rd time, hold your hand up, palm facing out.

Breathe. You got this. Do a fist pump to punctuate the final time.

Innovate

Use these 30 seconds to brainstorm new ideas to improve your workplace, your routine, or your job itself.

Thinking outside the box stimulates creativity and opens your mind to new ways to show your leadership abilities.

.

Find the Gem in the Junk

Criticism and negative feedback can hurt, but instead, can be a learning opportunity for self-improvement.

For 30 seconds, think of the last bit of criticism you received, dismiss the negativity, and find a tip for improvement that you can use.

If you find nothing useful, then give yourself a tip for dismissing empty negativity, take an assertive breath, and move on.

Wisdom Break

Access and express some of your accumulated wisdom. Surprise! You're wise!

Write your answers to:

3 things I've learned about supervising others.

Present Problems with Solutions

If you're going to bring up an issue, always have at least one potential solution ready to present with it. This shows you as a problem-solver rather than complainer, and opens a dialogue for productive change.

Start now by thinking of an inefficiency you know of, and at least one way to address it.

You've Come a Long Way, Baby!

This powerful reminder helps you realize your growth, and see your vast potential with fresh eyes.

Acknowledge your growth by listing, right now, three things you've learned in the past year.

If You Could

Imagine that you are designing the perfect job for you. Visualize what your workplace would look like, what you would be doing, wearing, who you would talk to, and what your work would be. Add as much detail as you can.

Afterward, compare this vision to your current circumstances.

- What actual steps can you take to bring the vision into your reality now?
- In a year?
- In five years?

Your Dream Job is Up to You

Imagine the career of your dreams.

> What skills do you already bring to that position?

> What do you still need to get there?

In this 30 seconds, make a list of steps. Creating this list helps you know it can be done.

Seeing it as doable helps you feel confident you can achieve it - **and you can.**

Get started!

Say Affirmations

To realign yourself with positive energy which attracts more goodness into your life, and helps increase optimism, say each of these aloud and with feeling:

Each day brings new opportunities to do great things.

Today is an awesome day.

I am ready to shine!

Act As If

Change your day by changing how you act.

Our actions actually cause our feelings to respond. Think: how would you act if you were having an awesome day? Would you walk with a bounce in your step? Smile big? Greet people with a friendly "Hello"?

Make a conscious effort to do these things and see how it changes how you feel - and your day.

Volunteer

Giving of time and skill is not only altruistic, it increases self-esteem, connects you with people, helps the world, helps you learn, and creates opportunities.

Find a cause, commit, and roll up your sleeves. The benefits outweigh monetary value every time.

Say Affirmations

To realign yourself with positive energy which attracts more goodness into your life, and helps increase optimism, say each of these aloud and with feeling:

I am innovative.

I have endless creative energy.

I tap into an unlimited flow of potential.

Wisdom Break

Access and express some of your accumulated wisdom. Surprise! You're wise! Write your answers to:

3 things I've learned about becoming good at what I do.

See Yourself Successful

What we create in our minds and expect to happen has a profound influence on our day.

Read this, close your eyes, then do it:

Picture in your mind: It's the end of the day today. You had a wonderful day. You were appreciated, productive, and easily successful in all you did. Imagine your happy and satisfied feeling. Feel It.

Then open your eyes and expect it's already in motion.

Be Real

The most recognized and successful people can admit to mistakes, say sorry, dream big, give credit, and laugh. You are special and important not only for what you can do, but for who you are. Be yourself and shine.

Use these 30 seconds to think about your most natural, human qualities, and appreciate them.

Say Affirmations

To realign yourself with positive energy which attracts more goodness into your life, and helps increase optimism, say each of these aloud and with feeling:

I attract prosperity easily.

I radiate with optimism.

I enjoy my work and it enriches my life.

Bring Out Your Happy

Focusing on things that make you happy helps you feel happier, and notice happy moments throughout your day.

Right now, list three little moments that made you happy today.

Was it the smell of coffee? The birds tweeting outside? A smile someone gave you? Nothing is too small to count. Afterward, be ready to notice the next one when it happens.

Wisdom Break

Access and express some of your accumulated wisdom. Surprise! You're wise!

Write your answers to:

3 things I've learned about getting a job.

Express Pride

It always feels good to hear that someone we work with is proud of us.

Think of a reason that you are proud of someone you work with - maybe it is an accomplishment, or the encouraging way your coworker treats others, or how attentive your coworker is to your clients or customers.

Whatever it is, be sure to express your pride in him or her today. Notice how good it feels to share this expression, and how its received.

Embrace Impulsivity

Unpredictability is great for igniting creativity and getting "unstuck."

Do something unusual today

Ideas: leave an anonymous note of encouragement on someone's desk, go to a new restaurant for lunch, read a new blog post on a website you've never looked at before.

In these 30 seconds, choose an idea and go for it!

Just for Today

No complaining.

If you feel like complaining, substitute the phrase, "At least it's not .... (something worse)" and let it go.

Notice the way your day changes when you lighten up.

See it Done

Think of your biggest goal for yourself. Take 30 seconds to visualize yourself having completed it. Let yourself really feel how great it would be to be there, with it accomplished.

Then, smile, knowing you've just sent a powerful order out to the Universe, and expect it to start coming into being.

Ask Yourself

Breathe for 10 seconds, and ask yourself:

What do I want to be remembered for?

Write your answer below.

Talk to Yourself

A great problem solving strategy is to talk yourself through a problem as if you are talking to your most trusted advisor.

For the next 30 seconds, close the door or go somewhere where you can be alone. Speak out loud to yourself about whatever's on your mind, and let your ideas flow.

Afterward, notice what sorts of insight you received, and be sure to give yourself credit for being capable of great insight.

Get Out of the Box

With only five skills, you can create any job or opportunity that you set your mind to.

These skills are:

- Read well
- Write well
- Do math
- Use a computer
- Be creative

If you're in need of skill-boosting in any of those areas, get it. There are tutorials available for free online, as well as free college classes you can take.

If not, think of how you can use these skills to move toward doing something that feels great to you. Maybe it's just a fun creative thing, or maybe it's an opportunity to make money or collaborate on a project you've always wanted to do.

Have a Real Conversation

Asking an open-ended question invites a true conversation. The next step is to listen fully to the answer.

Try "What do you think about _____," or "How do you feel about _____" as conversation openers that can help you engage in creative thinking with your coworkers or team, or just get to know the people you work with better.

Battle Buster

Sometimes many things can feel irritating. It can be tempting to lash out and vent a list of complaints. However, it's seldom productive to do so.

Think of your list of irritations, and then choose only those which can really be changed for the better right now.

Then, take one that you selected, and write three ways you can work toward improving the situation.

Yawn it Out

Yawning has the effect of bringing oxygen to the brain, stretching the jaw (thus releasing tension there), and clearing the mind.

Take a deep breath, and allow yourself to yawn – big – right now. Follow with a big stretch and a chest thump or two.

Aaaah! Refreshing.

Read and Share

When you learn something and then share it with someone, you increase your networking power, and show yourself to be a valuable resource in your business.

Go online and search or surf until you find something that you find interesting. Read it. Make a couple notes of the important points.

Then, think of someone you know who would also find this information useful.

Now, or later today, send an email, text, or give a call to this person, and share what you learned.

Wisdom Break

Access and express some of your
accumulated wisdom.
Surprise! You're wise!

In a notebook, write your answers to:

3 things I've learned about overcoming challenges.

ABOUT THE AUTHOR

Alice Langholt is a Reiki Master Teacher, the Executive Director of Reiki Awakening Academy School of Intuitive Development (ReikiAwakeningAcademy.com),  and the founder of Practical Reiki, a strong, simple Reiki energy healing method.

Alice is the author of the award-winning book, *Practical Reiki for balance, well-being, and vibrant health, A guide to a strong, revolutionary energy healing method*, and *The Practical Reiki Companion* workbook, as well as three apps, the *A Moment for Me 365 Day Self Care Calendar for Busy People*, and other books in the A Moment for Me series. (AMoment4Me.com).

She's passionate about finding and teaching simple approaches to strengthening intuition and achieving holistic balance.

Alice lives with her husband and their four children in Gaithersburg, Maryland.

She teaches Practical Reiki and other holistic topics, and offers workshops on 30 second methods of self-care online and in the Washington, DC area.

Contact Alice by email at Alice@AliceLangholt.com.